D1404827

A Child Is Born
The Story of the First Christmas

Mary Alice Gran

Abingdon Press
Nashville

A Child Is Born
The Story of the First Christmas

Copyright © 2008 by Abingdon Press
All rights reserved.

No part of this work may be reproduced or transmitted in any form or by any means, electronic or mechanical, including photocopying
and recording, or by any information storage or retrieval system, except as may be expressly permitted by the 1976 Copyright Act or by
permission in writing from the publisher. Requests for permission should be submitted in writing to:
Rights and Permissions, The United Methodist Publishing House,
201 Eighth Avenue, South, P.O. Box 801, Nashville, TN 37202-0801;
faxed to 615-749-6128; or submitted via e-mail to *permissions@abingdonpress.com*.

Unless otherwise noted, Scripture quotations are from the New Revised Standard Version of the Bible,
copyright 1989, Division of Christian Education of the National Council of the Churches of Christ
in the United States of America. Used by permission. All rights reserved.

ISBN 13: 978-0-687-49168-1

08 09 10 11 12 13 14 15 16 17—10 9 8 7 6 5 4 3 2 1

Printed in China

To all children,
each a gift of God to the world.

To my grandchildren:
Will, Kody, Carson, Cooper, and Hazel

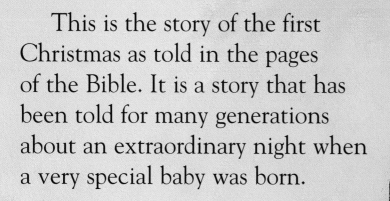

This is the story of the first Christmas as told in the pages of the Bible. It is a story that has been told for many generations about an extraordinary night when a very special baby was born.

It is a story that began many generations earlier when the prophet Isaiah gave the people a promise from God. He told them that a child would be born for them, a son given to them; and he would be called Wonderful Counselor, Mighty God, Everlasting Father, Prince of Peace.

For a child has been born for us,
a son given to us;
authority rests upon his shoulders;
and he is named
Wonderful Counselor, Mighty God,
Everlasting Father, Prince of Peace.

Isaiah 9:6

The story is centered two thousand years ago in the country of Israel where there were rock-covered hills and mountains, lonely villages, and the busy city of Jerusalem. At that time the Israelites were ruled by the Romans. Life was not easy.

Mary lived in the town of Nazareth. She was young in age, but her faith in God was strong and sure. One day she was visited by an angel who said, "Mary, you are a faithful servant of God. You are favored by God and have been chosen to give birth to a baby, the Son of God, the Prince of Peace."

Mary was confused. She was engaged to Joseph, the carpenter, and was not yet married. What would Joseph say? Would he still want her as his wife?

When Mary told Joseph the news of the baby, he was greatly troubled. He loved Mary. But how could it be that Mary was to have a baby? What was he to do?

That night while he was sleeping, the angel said to Joseph in a dream, "Joseph, do not be afraid to take Mary as your wife. The baby comes from God as a gift to the world. You are to name him Jesus."

Now the time came when the Roman Emperor, Caesar Augustus, declared that all people would register in the hometown of their family. Because Joseph was in the family of King David, he needed to travel to Bethlehem to be registered.

It would be a difficult trip, especially since Mary was soon to give birth. But they had to go. So Joseph and Mary traveled from Nazareth to Bethlehem.

Mary and Joseph arrived
in Bethlehem tired and
hungry, looking for a place
to stay. But other travelers
had arrived first and there
was no place left for them.
Finally an innkeeper offered
a stable where they would
be safe and warm.

While they were
there, Mary gave
birth to a son.
The Christ Child
had come! The
Prince of Peace
was born! The
prophecy of Isaiah
was fulfilled! Mary
wrapped baby Jesus in
strips of cloth and laid
him in the manger.

In a dark field nearby, shepherds were caring for their sheep. Suddenly an angel appeared. They were surrounded with light from the angel and were very frightened.

"Do not fear!" the angel said, "I am bringing you good news of great joy. Today in Bethlehem, a baby is born who is the Savior, the Messiah! You will find the baby wrapped in cloth and lying in a manger."

Suddenly the night sky was filled with angels saying, "Glory to God in the highest!"

When the angels had gone, the shepherds went in search of the new baby. They wanted to see what the angels had told them. Hurrying as fast as they could, they searched until they found Mary and Joseph, and the baby.

The shepherds told Mary and Joseph
about the angels and all that had happened.
When they left, they were praising God
for everything they had experienced.
Mary treasured all the shepherds had said,
keeping their words in her heart.

A bright star was being watched by some very wise
men. Traveling from a distant land in the East, they
followed the star as it moved across the sky toward
Jerusalem. They were dressed like kings and were called
Magi. They searched for the child who was born
to be King of the Jews.

When word of the Magi and their search reached King Herod, he was alarmed. Herod asked the chief priests and scribes about a new king. They told him of an old prophecy that said a king would be born in Bethlehem.

Meeting with
the Magi, King
Herod told them
to go to Bethlehem.
He said to the Magi,
"Tell me when you
have found this
new king. I want to
honor the child."
But in his heart,
he was worried that
the child would
take his place as
King of the Jews.

The Magi set out for Bethlehem. They were delighted when they saw the star was still leading the way. They were headed in the right direction and would soon find the new King.

When the star stopped over the place where the child was, they were overwhelmed with great joy. Entering the house, they found Mary and the Christ Child. Kneeling before the child, they opened their treasure chests to offer gifts of gold, fine perfume, and expensive oil—special gifts for a very special child.

When the Magi left, they did not tell King Herod where the child was as they traveled home by another route.

And the child Jesus grew in wisdom and strength.

In those days a decree went out from Emperor Augustus that all the world should be registered. . . . Joseph also went from the town of Nazareth in Galilee to Judea, to the city of David called Bethlehem, because he was descended from the house and family of David. He went to be registered with Mary, to whom he was engaged and who was expecting a child. While they were there, the time came for her to deliver her child. And she gave birth to her firstborn son and wrapped him in bands of cloth, and laid him in a manger, because there was no place for them in the inn.

Luke 2:1–7

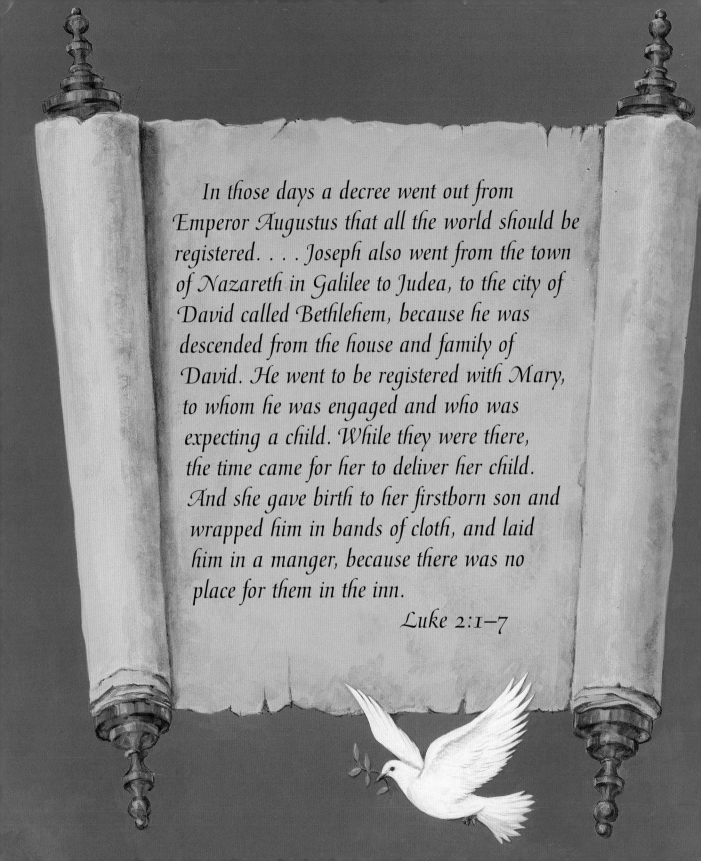